ORACLE QUICK GUIDES
PART 1 - THE BASICS
DATABASE & TOOLS

Malcolm Coxall

Edited by Guy Caswell

Cornelio
Books

Published by M.Coxall - Cornelio Books
Copyright 2013 Malcolm Coxall
First Published in Spain, United Kingdom 2013
ISBN: 978-84-941783-5-1

"Space does not exist unless there are objects in it

Nor does time exist without events."

Contents

Preface and Audience

Oracle Quick Guides: Welcome to Oracle Quick Guides, a series of quick learning guides for Oracle designers, developers and managers.

Guide Audience: These guides are designed to rapidly deliver key information about Oracle to the following audience groups:

- Project Managers, Team Leaders and Testers who are new to Oracle and need rapid access to strategic information about the Oracle development environment.

- Business Analysts, Designers and Software Developers who are new to Oracle and need to make a first step in gaining a detailed understanding of the design and development issues involved in Oracle.

Guide Contents: These guides have been divided by subject matter. They become increasingly complex and more specific the later the volume. Thus, volume 1 is quite general but later volumes are very technical and specific.

Our Objective: There are plenty of Oracle textbooks on the market. Most of them are huge and only partly relevant to a particular group of readers. Therefore, we decided to divide the subject into smaller, more targeted volumes in order that you only get the information YOU need.

For example, a Project Manager doesn't need to know some of the more esoteric programming tips but will need to know some of the strategic issues affecting design and testing. In a similar way, a Programmer is much more interested in the syntactic details than in the strategic issues affecting the choice of an Oracle upgrade path.

And so we target these guides at particular groups, with specific interests and we try to avoid overloading the reader with too much detail or extraneous material.

---oOo---

1. Oracle - A Brief History

Here are some nuggets from Oracle's history:

Oracle Corporation is an American multinational computer technology corporation headquartered in Redwood, California, United States.

Founder: Larry Ellison, a co-founder of Oracle Corporation, has served as Oracle's CEO throughout its history. On August 22, 2008, the Associated Press ranked Ellison as the highest paid chief executive in the world.

Products: Oracle specialises in developing and marketing computer hardware systems and enterprise software products - particularly its own brands of database management systems and tools. Oracle also builds tools for database development and systems of middle-tier software, such as Enterprise Resource Planning software (ERP), Customer Relationship Management software (CRM) and Supply Chain Management (SCM) software, to name just a small part of the Oracle applications portfolio.

Global Size: At the time of writing (2013) Oracle is the third-largest software maker by revenue, after Microsoft and IBM.

Timeline of Oracle's History

- **1970:** Paper written by Edgar F. Codd on relational database management systems (RDBMS) named "A Relational Model of Data for Large Shared Data Banks." This paper provides inspiration to Larry Ellison in his interest in large database design.

- **1977:** Larry Ellison co-founds Oracle Corporation in 1977 with Bob Miner and Ed Oates under the name Software Development Laboratories (SDL).

- **1978:** Oracle version 1, written in assembly language, runs in 128K of memory.

- **1979:** SDL changes its name to Relational Software, Inc. (RSI).

- **1979:** Oracle version 2 is released - the first commercial SQL RDBMS

- **1982:** RSI renames itself Oracle Systems Corporation to align itself more closely with its flagship product Oracle Database.

- **1983:** Oracle Database is rewritten in C for portability. Oracle is offered as VAX-mode database

- **1983:** Oracle version 3 is released.

- **1984:** Oracle version 4 is released as first database to offer read consistency.

- **1984:** Oracle database software is ported to the PC platform.

- **1986:** Oracle for MSDOS version 5 is released. Oracle version 5 is one of the first RDBMS to operate in client-server mode.

- **1986:** Oracle version 5.1 is released with support for distributed queries. Investigations into clustering begin. Oracle goes public.

- **1987:** Oracle founds its Applications division, building business-management software closely integrated with its database software, in UNIX environment.

- **1988:** Oracle version 6 is released. This has support for row-level locking and hot backups. The developers embed the PL/SQL procedural language into the database. Users could submit PL/SQL blocks for immediate execution in the server from an environment such as SQL*Plus, or via SQL statements embedded in a host program. Oracle included separate PL/SQL engines in various client tools (such as SQL*Forms and Reports).

- **1992:** Oracle 7 is released with performance enhancements, administrative utilities, application-development tools, security features, the ability to persist PL/SQL program units in the database as stored procedures and triggers, and support for declarative referential integrity.

- **1993:** Oracle releases its "Cooperative Development Environment" (CDE), which bundles Oracle Forms, Reports, Graphics, and Book.

- **1995:** Oracle Corporation announces new data-warehousing facilities, including parallel queries and offers the first 64-bit RDBMS.

- **1996:** Oracle releases Web Browser of the Oracle Power Browser and moves towards an open standards-based, web-enabled architecture.

- **1997:** Oracle releases the first version of Discoverer.

- **1997:** Oracle 8 is released with SQL object technology, Internet technology and support for terabytes of data.

- **1997:** Oracle Corporation announces a commitment to the Java platform, and introduces Oracle's Java integrated development environment JDeveloper.

- **1998:** Oracle releases Oracle Applications 10.7 Network Computing Architecture (NCA). All the applications in the business software now run across the web in a standard web browser.

- **1998:** Oracle Corporation releases Oracle Applications 11.

- **1998:** Oracle 8*i* is released (the 'i' stands for Internet).

- **1998:** Oracle 8 and Oracle Application Server 4.0 are released on the Linux platform.

- **1999:** Offers its first DBMS with XML support

- **2000:** Oracle 9*i* and Application Server is released.

- **2004:** Oracle 10*g* is released (the *g* stands for Grid - "Enterprise Grid Computing").

- **2004:** Oracle takes control of PeopleSoft.

- **2005:** Oracle takes control of Siebel Systems.

- **2005:** Oracle releases its first free database, Oracle Database 10*g* Express Edition.

- **2006:** Oracle APEX development environment is introduced.

- **2007:** Oracle 11*g* is released.

- **2010:** Oracle acquires Sun Microsystems

- **2012:** The Oracle database is available on the following platforms:
  - zLinux64
  - Microsoft Windows (32-bit)
  - Microsoft Windows (x64)

- o   Linux x86
- o   Linux x86-64
- o   Solaris (SPARC) (64-bit)
- o   Solaris (x86-64)
- o   HP-UX Itanium
- o   HP-UX PA-RISC (64-bit)
- o   AIX (PPC64)

- **2013:** At the time of writing Oracle is ranked at 82nd on the Fortune 500 Largest Corporations with revenues just under $36 billion in 2011.

---oOo---

2. Relational databases: An introduction

2.1 Introduction: Oracle has become an immensely successful company because it has built its business around a unique type of database structure - the Relational database. Relational databases deliver extraordinary productivity gains when handling large amounts of data and the introduction of relational databases has revolutionised data management in the last 25 years.

Oracle's entire product line centres on the relational database. Therefore, it is really important for everyone involved in any Oracle project to understand the basic concepts of this relational database. Not only do the structures of a relational database alter the methodology of analysis and design of the data store but it also alters the way software is designed, built and tested.

So, whether you are a business user, a project manager, a business analyst, software designer, developer, systems administrator or database administrator, it is vital that you understand the basic rules that govern relational database technology.

2.2 What is a Relational database?

2.2.1 Definition of a Relational database:

- A relational database is a collection of data items organized as a set of formally described tables from which data can be accessed easily.

- A relational database is created using the relational model.

- The software used in a relational database is called a relational database management system (RDBMS).

2.2.2 The Relational Model: This is the logical model used to define data and relationships between data. It is used by a relational database and has various elements. The single most important characteristic is that it is capable of modelling the natural relationships between datasets in an efficient way without data redundancy. For example, a relational model defines fixed structures for data stores and it also defines and constrains the relationship between any two sets of data and how data is uniquely identified.

So what makes this different from a flat data-storage used by a traditional 3G language?

In non-relational data storage environments, rules for whether a data element is optional, for defining and enforcing relationships with other data stores, for data element validation, and guaranteeing of uniqueness would all be enforced using programmatic code etc. This means that during insert, update and delete processes a whole range of data validation must be executed to enforce all the possible validation and transactional rules affecting the data sets being transacted.

However, in a relational database environment, all of these rules (and many more) can be defined as an intrinsic part of the database definitions. This means that these rules become implicit parts *of the database itself.* Thereafter, these rules are guaranteed by the relational database instance, meaning that no code is required to manage the basic data entry validation needed to enforce these rules. The database takes cares of these fundamental business constraints without further programmatic intervention and can therefore also guarantee the referential integrity of the database against both bad data and external threats to the data itself from poor code etc.

2.3 The Relational Model - Early Research: In his original research work for IBM, mathematician Edgar Codd recognised that data which was *related* to other data could be stored and accessed more efficiently than in the simple sequential strings used in the 3G programming languages. These sequential strings were basically randomly designed and held no intrinsic relational structures - they were just fixed format "data dumps" where data could be stored, updated, deleted and retrieved but little else.

Codd saw the intrinsic relationships between data. For example, he reasoned that a single invoice had many invoice lines and that therefore a "one to many" relationship existed between an invoice and its invoice lines. He correctly calculated that an understanding of these relationships could be used to structure and identify strings of data uniquely, together with their relationships to other data and that this could radically improve the efficiency of data storage and retrieval by eliminating duplication of data in the data store.

The following diagram illustrates the underlying relationships within a simple invoice:

INVOICE

Date:	10-AUG-2011
Invoice No:	2313413
Customer:	VILLAGE COOP
	THE VILLAGE COOPERATIVE
Tax ID:	786876786786DF
Address:	THE VILLAGE COOPERATIVE
	Bempton
	Y02 768H Ripon, North Yorkshire

Invoice Header (1)

Invoice Lines (many)

Product Code	Product Name	Qty	Price / Un	Disı %
JAM003	TOMATO CHUTNEY 0.5KG	200.00	2.00	0
JAM004	BLACKCURRANT JAM 0.5KG - ORGANIC	11.00	2.00	0
JAM005	RHUBARB JAM 0.5KG	150.00	2.00	0
JAM007	CHERRY JAM 0.5KG	25.00	2.00	0
TRANSPORT	TRANSPORT UNIT COST 10 POUNDS	1.00	10.00	0

Codd realised that data need only be stored *once* but could be referred to *many times*. In the invoice example, he realised that all the invoice "header" data (such as customer, address, invoice date, invoice number etc) didn't need to be stored with every invoice line (product id, invoice quantity, tax rate etc) and that it was sufficient simply to relate invoice line data to their appropriate *parent* invoice header data. In this case, the unique Invoice No could be used to define the relationship between the Invoice lines and the Invoice header.

Behind Codd's research was a complex mathematical reasoning which is not the subject of this volume. However, Codd's conclusions formed the basis of the so-called "Manifestos" of relational databases, which are the basis of modern RDBMS like Oracle.

2.4 Relational Terminology and Concepts: Let's look a bit further at how relational theory translates into a real relational database. In order to do this we need to understand a few basic words and concepts used in relational database design and theory:

2.4.1 Logical and Physical Design: To get to grips with the terminology used in relational databases it's important to understand the basic flow of database design and build.

In relational database technology, analysis and design is everything. Getting the data model properly defined is critical to the correct workings of a relational database. There are several proprietary tools available to assist in the analysis and design of a relational database. Oracle has several products. The traditional product is Oracle Designer. Non-Oracle products also exist including Toad and Erwin. They all basically do the same thing. In all of these Quick Guides, we will focus on using Oracle Designer v10, since it is the predominantly recommended Oracle CASE product, for now at least. These are the basic steps in the Analysis and Design of an Oracle database:

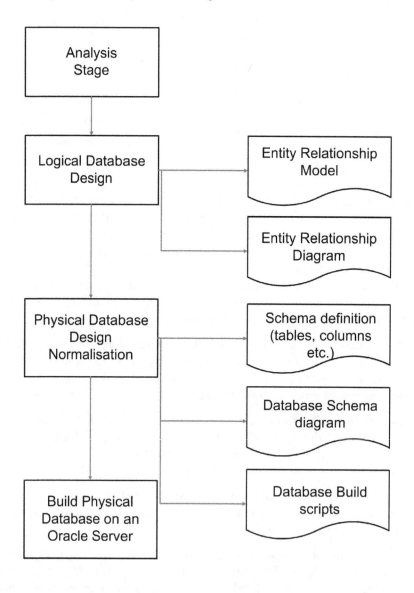

The two main definition steps in relational database development are Analysis and Design which have the following outputs

- Analysis stage will give rise to an Entity Relationship (E-R) model and an E-R Diagram. These are then used by the database designer to normalise the data to remove redundancy and database anomalies.

- Design stage will give rise to a Physical Database Design, Schema Diagram and database build scripts which are then used to build the physical database and its component object in a real Oracle database instance.

The Analysis stage will seek to produce a "Logical Data model" consisting of complete logical definitions of entities, attributes and relationships.

The Design stage will use the logical model as its basis and then, using a process of normalisation (which we will explain later), the designer will convert logical definitions (entities, attributes, relationships, unique identifiers, etc) into a physical database definition (tables, columns, constraints, keys etc.) ready to be built and used on an Oracle Server. The physical design will contain definitions of all the database objects required to build the physical database and will be capable of generating the code to build these database objects.

2.4.2 Equivalent Terms: The following terms are equivalent in Logical and Physical Database design:

Logical Term	Physical Database Object	Meaning
Entity	Table	A fixed database structure where data is stored, like an Invoice Headers or Employees table.
Attribute	Column	A single element of a table. For example, an invoice number column, where invoice numbers are stored within a table.

Logical Term	Physical Database Object	Meaning
Occurrence	Record	One single data record, unique in a database.
Unique Identifier	Unique Key / Primary Key	A column (or group of columns) which uniquely identifies just one record in a table, for example, an invoice number may identify just one invoice.
Relationship	Foreign Key Constraint	A column (or group of columns) which are part of a record but which relate it to a foreign table. For example, in an Invoice Header table, a Customer id is used to relate the invoice to one single Customer in the Customers table.
E-R model and E-R diagram	Schema design and schema diagram	A Schema design and diagram represents the *physical* database design which results from the normalisation of a logical entity relationship model.

Entity-Relationship model: This is a way of describing a relational database in terms of where and how data is stored and the relationships between different data. An E-R model consists of data definitions and relationships and often results in a schematic representation of a database called an E-R diagram.

Entity: An entity is something which is recognized as being capable of an independent existence and which can be uniquely identified. For example, an invoice header is an entity which can be uniquely identified by an Invoice No. In a physical database, an Entity is equivalent to a Table, in which a particular dataset is stored.

Attributes: An attribute is a component of an entity. For example, an Invoice Header has the following attributes: Invoice No., Invoice Date, Customer Id, etc. In a physical database, an Attribute is equivalent to a Column in a table.

Relationships: Data in one entity may be related to data in another entity. A relationship is expressed as a verb. So for example, an invoice *consists of* several invoice lines. Invoice and invoice line are the entities and "consists of" is the relationship. A relationship in a physical database is manifested as a Foreign Key Constraint, which provides a link between a "parent" record and one or more "child" records.

Cardinality: Several relationships are possible. In data modelling, the cardinality of one data table with respect to another data table is a critical aspect of database design. Relationships between data tables define cardinality when explaining how each table links to another.

In the relational model, entities can be related as any of:

- One-to-one.

- One-to-many (or many-to-one).

- Many-to-many.

This is said to be the cardinality of a given entity in relation to another. The relationship between an Invoice Header and Invoice Lines is said to be a one to many relationship.

E-R Diagrams: These are especially useful for defining a schematic view of a relational database, its entities, and relationships. There are several conventions used, but the most popular is the so-called "Crows-Foot" diagram which is also used in Oracle's Designer tools. We will discuss this technique in more detail later.

Here is an example of an E-R diagram to show the relationship between Orders and Order Lines:

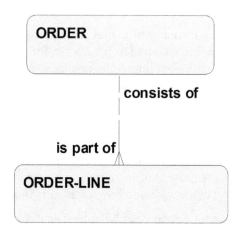

E-R Diagram interpretation: Note that the E-R Diagram refers to the entities in the singular. It shows the verbs used to express the relationships between the two entities and it also shows the cardinality of the relationship using the crow's foot. The dotted end of the relationship line indicates that an order header can exist without an order line. An order line is said to be optional. However, an order line cannot exist without an order header.

Unique identifiers: In his relational view of the world, Codd could see that personal data such as name, date of birth, gender, social security number (what we call "attributes") were sometimes specific to just one individual person but sometimes they were not. His treatise reasoned that there may be thousands of John Smiths, so obviously "name" or "date of birth" alone would not be a good way to find one particular John Smith. And thus, he realised that data for one particular individual could only really be *absolutely* uniquely accessed by some "key" data which was completely unique to that person. This key data was referred to as a *unique key* or *unique identifier*.

So, in our example, a social security number is unique and therefore would be a good unique identifier to find the record for one specific "John Smith". Codd also recognised that there may be more than one unique identifier for a person and that maybe a combination of other personal attributes may be considered unique for a person, such as "place of birth", "surname", and "date of birth", if they are all taken together to identify one person. These unique combinations could, he reasoned, also be considered "unique identifiers" if they truly are unique to the person in question. In a physical database unique identifiers become manifested as Unique Key Constraints. One of the unique keys is chosen as a Primary Key and manifested as a Primary Key Constraint for a particular table.

Normalisation: One of the underlying mathematical principles in Codd's relational theory is that of normalisation of data. In relational database design, normalisation is a process which takes place during and after the process of Entity-Relationship modelling, where a logical data model is being transformed into a physical data model before being turned into a physical database.

Despite being so fundamental to relational design, data normalisation is still widely misunderstood by Users, Analysts, Designers and Developers.

The primary objectives of data normalisation are the removal of redundancy and dependency. This means that when data is inserted, updated or deleted, these processes only take place once in each table. Normalisation works by dividing large entities or tables into smaller (less redundant) entities (tables) and by amalgamating entities together which have a shared one-to one relationship.

There are three concepts of data normalisation referred to as "first, second and third normal form". Generally speaking, the objective of a relational database designer is to define a database which conforms to "Third Normal Form". However, there are many exceptions to this objective which we will explore in a later chapter, when discussing database performance.

For now, here are the rules for each level of data normalisation:

- **First Normal Form** states that a "Table faithfully represents a relation, primarily meaning it has at least one candidate key". So, first normal form deals really with the "shape" of a record type. Under first normal form, all occurrences of a record type must contain the same number of fields. First normal form excludes repeating fields and groups. This basically means that repeating data must be removed from a table to eliminate repeating groups of data. Thus, if we had an Invoice table which incorporated invoice line and invoice header data in the same records, we would need to separate the data into two tables in order to make it conform to first normal form.

19

- **Second Normal Form** states that "no non-prime attribute in the table is functionally dependent on a proper subset of any candidate key". So, the objective here to bring data to 2nd Normal form is to remove part key dependents, the data that is *partly* dependent on a key. For example, in our invoice lines table, we would not include the attributes "Product price" or "Product description" because these attributes ought to be part of a separate "Products" table, if our database were normalised to 2nd Normal form.

- **Third Normal Form** states that every non-prime attribute is non-transitively dependent on every candidate key in the table. The attributes that do not contribute to the description of the primary key are removed from the table. In other words, no transitive dependency is allowed. The objective here is is to remove non key dependencies, i.e. data that is not dependent on other keys. So, are any of the attributes primarily dependent on one of the other non-key attributes rather than the design key? In our Invoice Header example, Customer Name, Address and Tax Id would be separated into a separate Customer table. Only the Customer number would appear in the Invoice Header table, and so on.

2.5 The benefits of the Relational database: The benefits of a relational database become very obvious when it comes to moving from a logical model to the physical database design. Here are the key benefits which are normally experienced:

2.5.1 Data is only stored once. The advantages of this are:

- No multiple record changes needed.

- More efficient storage.

- Simple to delete or modify details.

- All records in other tables having a link to that entry will show the change.

2.5.2 Complex queries can be carried out: A language called SQL has been developed to allow programmers to 'Insert', 'Update', 'Delete', 'Create', 'Drop' table records. These actions are further refined by a 'Where' clause. For example

    SELECT * FROM Customer WHERE CUST_ID = 2

This SQL statement will extract record number 2 from the Customer table. Far more complicated queries can be written that can extract data from many *related* tables at once. A simple example of a join within a query would be something like this:

```
SELECT * from ORDER_HEADER OH, CUSTOMER C
WHERE OH.CUST_REF = C.CUST_ID
AND C.CUST_ID = 2...
```

2.5.3 Supports set functions: Relational databases permit user-friendly data manipulation techniques, for example, set operations and relational algebra. They make complex data requests quite simple, because they allow query operations such as joins, unions, minus, correlated sub-queries. Oracle allows for the storage of view objects which embed complex pre-defined database queries, but which also can be simply queried by a non-expert user.

2.5.4 Better security: By splitting data into tables, certain tables can be made confidential. When a person logs on with their username and password, a relational database like Oracle can limit access only to those tables whose records they are authorised to view. For example, a receptionist would be able to view employee location and contact details but not their salary. A salesman may see his team's sales performance, but not competing teams'.

In addition, security can be defined at a table and functional level, with one user being able to update, but not insert to a particular table. This provides huge security benefits and flexibility.

2.5.5 Cater for future requirements: By having data held in separate tables, it is simple to add records that are not yet needed but may be needed in the future. For example, the city table could be expanded to include every city and town in the country, even though no other records are using them all as yet.

2.5.6 Business Rules are embedded within the database itself: With the advent of the so-called Object-Relational database, many of the fixed business rules of a data set can be embedded in the database itself. This saves a lot of validation coding and future code maintenance. This means that once a database has been properly defined and the "business rules" defining relationships and other data characteristics have been entered, the database becomes capable of defending itself against data which contradicts the business rules. In practice, the database will simply not allow invalid data to be written to it. For example, if we attempted to write 2 department records to the departments table with the same unique identifier, the database would simply reject the records by raising an error and rolling back the transaction. Or if we attempted to create an employee that didn't belong

21

to a valid department, again, the database would reject the record with an error. Why? Because, according to the business rules we defined, every employee MUST belong to a valid department. We defined this "constraint" in our database and the database enforces it without any additional code.

2.5.7 User interface software design and software code can be derived and generated from relational rules embedded in the database: Database relational and other constraints are embedded in a relational database such as Oracle. They are enforced by the database to "defend" the integrity of the database. However, once defined, these rules can also be used by various code generators to build user interfaces, which incorporate the embedded validation rules. Oracle Forms and Oracle APEX, for example, generates front-end software based on these relational rules. The front end software uses these rules to warn the user of an invalid entry. The use of automatic code generators such as Oracle Forms or Oracle APEX with this already generated validation code saves a significant amount of routine programmer effort and reduces testing risk and cost.

2.6 A closer look at types of relationship: We will now take a look at all of the possible relationships which can exist within a logical data model. We will review them in order of their complexity. A recursive relationship is just a variant of a "one to many" relationship but it is a bit more complicated so we will deal with it separately here.

2.6.1 The one to one relationship (1:1): This is where one occurrence of an entity relates to only one occurrence in another entity. A one-to-one relationship rarely exists in practice, but it can. However, you may consider combining them into one entity. Almost all one to one relationships are resolved by amalgamating the data into a single table. There are occasional exceptions made for performance reasons - but rarely.

For example, an employee is allocated a company car, which can only be driven by that employee. Therefore, there is a one-to-one relationship between employee and company car. A one to one relationship is represented as follows in an E-R diagram:

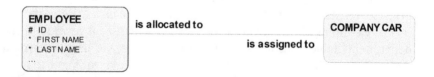

2.6.2 The one to many relationship (1: n and n:1): This is a relationship we have already encountered with our Invoice example. An invoice contains many invoice lines for the ordered products:

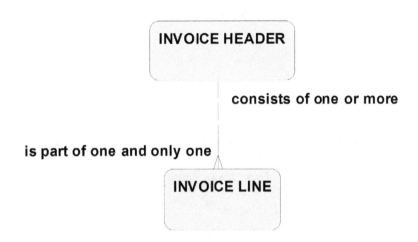

In nature and in business, there are many such "one to many" relationships. Orders have many order lines, bank accounts have many transactions, food products have many ingredients, hotels have many rooms etc. etc.

The one to many relationship is the basis of most business relational models and by far the most important relationship you will encounter in general data modelling. In normalising a logical data model with a "one to many" relationship, it is important to separate attributes according to the rules of 2nd and 3rd normal form by placing them in the correct table. So for example, an invoice line quantity would be associated with the Invoice line table and NOT the Invoice header table.

2.6.3 The many to many relationship (n:n): This is not an uncommon type of relationship. For example, let us consider a food company that makes a number of different finished products from a range of raw materials. Each finished product consists of a different combination of raw materials. But also, each raw material is used in several different finished products.

From a logical design point of view we can state:

- A Finished Product must contain one or many Raw Materials

AND

- A Raw Material may be used in one or many Finished Products

This can be represented as follows:

A many to many relationship cannot exist in a physical relational database, so, during normalisation, a many to many relationship is resolved by creating a so-called "intersect table" which contains the matching keys from both the original parent tables. Here a new Entity (table) called Finished-Product-Ingredient-List is created to resolve the n:n relationship as follows:

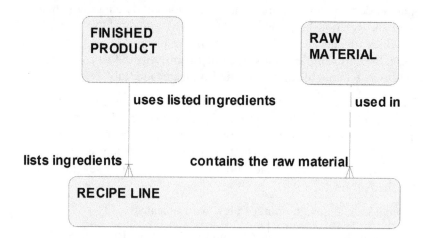

2.6.4 The recursive relationship (also called a "pig's ear") (1:n recursive): Sometimes data within an entity (table) is related to other data in the *same* table. This is not a very common relationship, but it is one that needs to be understood because it may be easily missed during analysis.

Taking a simple example, we could have a table of employees which contains all grades of employees including managers. These employees are identified using an EMPLOYEE_ID. Also, within this table we may include an attribute which indicates the EMPLOYEE_ID of each employee's manager. Every employee has a manager, so based on this we have a so-called recursive relationship, where one or more employees are related to another employee who is their manager. Or, from the employee-manager's perspective, each employee may be the manager of one or more other employees. This is represented as follows in an E-R or Schema diagram:

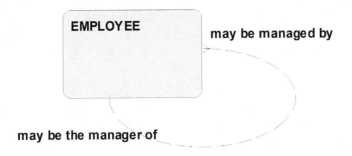

Recursive relationships are a little more complicated than relationships between two different tables (entities), but fundamentally they are the same as any other "one to many" relationship.

---o0o---

3. How relational databases impact software development.

3.1 Introduction: In a traditional 3G development environment, the storage of data takes place using a group of pre-defined "flat" file structures. These are basically operating system files that a developer defines and which the software uses to store data. The software is required to insert, update, delete data from these flat structures and allow data to be retrieved from them based on the user requirements of the software. In this kind of development environment, the software which manages the writing of data to these flat structures must also take care of implementing all rules for validation and a myriad other housekeeping tasks such as data read consistency, record locking etc.

The validation and processing tasks include allocating unique record identifiers to new records, validating new and updated records against existing data to prevent duplication, validating that a deletion does not cause the orphaning of related "child data", updating summary data (such as invoice totals) when data is inserted or updated, cross validation of data elements entered or changed by a user before an insert or update, etc. etc. The list is extensive.

In fact, most of the efforts of 3G designers and developers using flat file storage are expended in the design and development of basic data validation and management procedures, most of which are basically the same, but which have to be defined and coded separately. Worse still, the same kinds of validations need to be designed and coded for every flat file data store. This also creates a very complex set of maintenance dependencies. This in turn generates a rapidly expanding maintenance workload, as structural or functional changes require changes not only to flat file definitions, but also to a quantity of code and any dependent structures and code. Very rapidly, even fairly simple systems can become serious cost burdens as maintenance backlogs develop. Most 3G systems had associated maintenance costs many times greater than their initial capital costs.

Happily, the advent of relational databases such as Oracle has changed all this. They allowed most of the core business rules to be embedded in the database itself, thus eliminating most validation code. Oracle manages security implicitly at a totally granular level - defining which users can carry out what functions on what table and to which rows of data. Oracle also automatically manages data read and write consistency, guaranteeing that what you see is the latest version of the data. Oracle automatically manages table and record locking to guarantee that a transaction is completed before another one may begin in a multi-user environment, and Oracle rigorously defends the referential integrity of the data against the ingress of invalid data, i.e. if part of a transaction fails, the whole transaction is rolled back - thus preventing partial data corruption - the nightmare of the 3G designer and programmer.

However, there are some important considerations and restrictions which need to be considered in an Oracle environment and we will take a look at these in some detail now.

3.2 Comparison of 3G and Oracle Developments: There are 3 areas where significant differences exist between traditional 3G and Oracle development approach:

- Strategic issues, such as project methodologies, software engineering techniques.

- Practical design and development differences, such as approach to validation, locking, data consistency, security and software performance etc.

- Restrictions in development approach resulting from the imposition of the Oracle relational model.

3.2.1 Strategic issues in developing in an Oracle environment: There are a number of important differences in the approach to design and development between 3G software developments and developments in Oracle 7 and later versions. These differences exist because much of the functionality of a software system is pre-embedded in an Oracle database, whereas much of this functionality must be explicitly and painstakingly designed and developed in a 3G flat file environment. For a project manager, it's important to adapt the software design and management methodology to fit with the imperatives of relational database design, and not to stick rigidly to traditional approaches to software engineering such as SSADM etc.

3.2.1.1 Software Engineering Models:

3G developments rely on very long cycle Analysis-Design-Build methodologies such as the Waterfall model. This has very separate and distinct phases of specification and development. The reason for this is that any errors in specification or design can have huge implications on structures and software in dependent parts of an application. This risk of a design failure is so great, that huge emphasis is placed on meticulous analysis and design of structures and process flows, including many basic validations. In this environment almost the very last action to take place is coding of the software to implement the requirements and detailed design. This carries with it the risk that after a long period of system definition, the resulting software is either redundant or fails to match the user requirements. These risks are inherent in long-cycle software engineering methodologies, where perhaps 80% of the project effort goes into analysis and detailed software design and only 20% of the effort into development and testing.

Oracle developments, on the other hand, tend to support much shorter cycle methodologies such as Rapid Application Development (RAD). In RAD a "Designer-Builder" can move rapidly from a logical user requirements statement into a physical prototyping environment. The use of multiple recursive development cycles can be employed to evaluate user requirements and changes and to quickly prove them or reject them in the design. This short design-build cycle is made possible, because much of the hard work of managing basic business rules is actually already done as soon as the database is fully designed and built. Issues such as data consistency, data security, and locking are already built in.

These "in-built" features and database characteristics relieve the process and the programmer of the enormous overheads of code design, repetitive coding, and unit testing. Because these business rules are stored and executed within the database itself as separate objects, this also means that the risk of contagious knock-on effects of design failures on other dependent structures or code is very much more limited. So even if a design failure occurs, it will be confined to one or two tables; it does not unravel an entire software design and it is generally simple to resolve within the standard RAD design-build iterative process. This has major cost and delivery implications. It also should make a project manager realise the vital importance of getting the initial database design absolutely right as soon as possible, before proceeding to a cycle of software builds. The less faults in the database design, the less software design and build failures later.

3.2.1.2 - Practical design and development differences such as approach to validation, locking, data consistency, security and software performance etc.

New 3G entrants to the relational world sometimes find it hard to take on board the concept that not everything has to be coded. After all, that's what 3G programmers do. So it comes as a bit of a shock that much of what they needed to code in the past is no longer necessary. Instead, much of the effort that used to go into 3G design and coding is translated into good upfront database design. Getting a good, realistic and resilient logical and physical database design together is certainly the single greatest priority in this environment. Why is this?

In Oracle (and other relational DB environments) data is stored in a number of related tables. But these tables are not just storage "devices", they exhibit some intelligence as well, given to them by the database designer and so, each table acts as a fairly autonomous, semi-intelligent object. When we define a database, we define not only table structures, but also primary and unique key constraints to guarantee record uniqueness, foreign keys to constrain relationships with other tables. We may define check constraints to validate and constrain the relationship between data in the same row of a table or with rows in any other tables. The business rules which can be defined within a relational database are literally limitless.

Not only does the database validate and constrain the data which can be inserted, updated and deleted in a form of latent validation, but we can also build database objects which execute active database transactions. These database triggers, as they are called, are small autonomous tracts of code, which can be executed conditionally when various database events take place. They occur simultaneously when the database event occurs. If the main event fails or the "cascading" trigger code fails, then the entire transaction is rolled back - thus data consistency is maintained. So for example, adding a new INVOICE LINE record could be made to always "trigger" off a cascading POST INSERT trigger, which then automatically updates the INVOICE HEADER table with a new Invoice total value.

This encapsulation of relational and other validation into the database and the use of database triggers is, of course alien to a 3G developer, who sees storage objects such as flat files - as completely "dumb" objects. This demands that the entire emphasis of the programmer moves towards a much more *data-centric* approach. An Oracle developer must therefore also become intimately familiar with the design of the database at a very granular level.

In addition to this, Oracle also has built-in record and table locking, read consistency and security. This means that the programmer can effectively forget about these issues. So, for example, when a record is being updated by another user, it is held in a locked state by that user. Other users can see the data in its old form (because the update hasn't yet been committed to the database), but other users are unable to update that record until the first user is finished with the transaction. This system of FIFO locking guarantees the read consistency of the data in the database. In a similar way, the structure of users and roles within Oracle provides a system of user administration at the lowest level of the database. Very specific privileges can be granted to a user or a group of users to ensure that what they can see and do is what is allowed. This security operates at table, row and even column level for a specific user and a specific function such as INSERT, UPDATE, DELETE, SELECT. All of this functionality is effectively transparent to the developer, and rarely is it necessary for a developer to be involved in either security or data read consistency.

3.2.1.3 Restrictions in development approach resulting from the imposition of the Oracle relational model

On the downside (perhaps), development in a relational environment means that the rules of the database structures are extremely inflexible. A developer in a relational environment must understand the embedded business rules; otherwise the developer will certainly come into conflict with the constraints embedded in the Oracle database structure at some point during development.

No coding around constraints: For example, 3G programmers have many ways of taking shortcuts to force data to be stored or to by-pass validations in "exceptional" circumstances. This approach just won't work in a relational environment. The database is unforgiving and inflexible. So, for example, if data doesn't match the constraints in a table, then the data will be rejected and an exception will be raised. Short of altering the table design (which is effectively impossible in a running application), there is no way that violating data will ever be committed to a constrained table. This rigidity can be frustrating to a traditional programmer who is used to coding around restrictions (also known as hacking!). There is no coding around an Oracle database constraint.

Locking and Read consistency in an internet environment: As in other databases of flat file storage systems, building a transactional application which works in the "stateless" environment of the internet can present some challenges, particularly with regard to record locking and read consistency of data. The issue is no less complex in Oracle.

In a Client-Server environment, a persistent connection exists between a single logged in client and the database application on the server. In this condition, Oracle takes and holds a "row-level" lock against any record which is being updated (or deleted), thus ensuring that no other user can update that particular record at the same time. If the connection is broken or the transaction is abandoned by the user, these locks are released and other users may then update the data.

In a web-based software environment, there is generally no persistent connection between the web browser client based on html and the database server. (Oracle Forms v6i upwards does provide such a persistent connection, but it is rarely used in a web-based development). Normally, data is first retrieved by the user web application from the server database. It is then altered by the remote user and then posted back to the database. However, in the time between retrieving the data and posting it back again, anything could have happened to the data. For example, another user may have retrieved the same rows and deleted them or altered them in a different way. This gives rise to the potential for data becoming inconsistent or corrupted.

However, Oracle does provide methods of explicitly locking just the rows currently being queried by a user using the "for update" syntax in the underlying SQL select statement. This provides a possibility to allow read-only access to other users during an update or delete transaction by the first user. In fact, the "for update" solution is a particularly simple way of solving this problem which many other database or flat file development environments do not provide. So in this respect, Oracle manages this problem rather well. We will discuss the detailed use of this technique and concepts of optimistic and pessimistic locking strategies in a later volume.

Performance issues: Other restrictions which a developer finds in working in an Oracle environment include the impact of their code on the performance of an Oracle query or transaction. Oracle performance is a complex issue involving database instance configuration, physical database design, and good SQL software design. We will deal with the subject in a later volume of these guides. However, from a developer's point of view, failing to pay attention to the structure of SQL code being used or the underlying database design can cause some really catastrophic performance issues. A programmer without sufficient skills can write SQL code to cause a query to make full table scans across multiple joined tables containing trillions of record combinations. So, again, the programmer needs to move away from a focus on simple coding to a good understanding of how the database processes a SQL query or transaction and this means having a good understanding of the relational structure of the particular database itself.

Unit and System Testing issues: Testing in an Oracle environment is a fairly predictable business, because most of the functionality exists in small blocks of code in fairly atomic locations such as a single table constraint for "duplicate primary key". These are easy unit tests to script and execute.

Also, many of the elements which might require unit and system testing in a relational database are effectively eliminated because they are built in to the Oracle environment and can be taken as read (locking and user security testing for example). However, even if locking and user security are explicitly tested as part of a unit and system test regime, it is quite a simple matter to build a matrix of standard tests to be applied against all pieces of software and database objects. The issues involving table and row locking are well known and it is easy to establish relevant tests to ensure that these regimes are working in both positive and negative testing environments. This is also true of the basic business validations and the testing of cascading transactions.

In a 3G environment, the testing challenge is much greater because fundamental infrastructures such as read consistency and locking may compound other functional tests and may create complex interferences between tests.

3.2.1.4 Human Resource issues affecting Oracle developments: Depending on the software engineering methodology adopted (RAD or a more traditional "waterfall type" process), it is important to consider some of the HR issues that impact on successful Oracle developments. The following issues are relevant:

3.2.1.4.1 Skills choice. This is obviously vital to assembling a good design and development team. But, beware; Oracle creates its own HR selection priorities. One rule should be observed in all HR selections: Do not employ personnel who have no Oracle experience. It may seem obvious, but it is amazing how many project managers labour under the fallacy that Oracle is "just another development environment, no different to any other". This can be a traumatic and costly error of judgement.

Analysts - Designers: In a more traditional 3G environment, an analyst was an analyst, regardless of the language being used or the data storage strategy of the development. That changes radically with the relational datamodel, because the Oracle Analyst-Designer really needs to understand both the general Object-Relational philosophy, and also needs to understand the limitations and possibilities of the Oracle RDBMS. This is essential to develop a successful strategy for the delivery of the user's requirements. In this respect, Oracle is quite a unique environment.

Therefore, it is really important to choose personnel with solid Oracle experience. For example, traditional SSADM-type business analysts will not understand the embedded nature of Oracle's validation flow, for example, its DML-event driven trigger execution. A traditional business analyst would probably see "data validation" as a "process" rather than an intrinsic "property" of a database object. Therefore, it is crucial to employ skills which have appropriate hands-on Oracle experience and understanding of the required design and development approach. Oracle (along with other relational database systems) has a totally different paradigm to more traditional software developments.

Development DBA Group: This is the single most important group in any Oracle development. They should have a mature understanding of the relational model, the Oracle tools being used and the management of an Oracle design and development in a multi-user environment. These DBAs should be able to train, mentor and control analysts and designers and help with advice on quality SQL coding, performance management and providing visibility of the physical data model to the Designer-Builders.

Front-end Designer- Builders: Front end programmers need to have enough skills in Oracle to understand the vagaries of relational databases and how SQL coding impacts on performance and data returns (data sets, their formatting etc.). It's better to have a propensity towards database programmers with one or two high quality front end designer-builders. A beautiful web page can belie a totally disastrous back end.

3.2.1.4.2 Division and Organisation of Labour - In general, more effort is expended in database design in an Oracle development than in actual front end coding. This is often the reverse of a 3G development, where data storage is of almost no consequence. This will obviously impact on the crewing levels for different skills. An Oracle software development must have at least one Development DBA to take charge of the development database. This is a key skill and should have the responsibility to manage and approve all database changes during a development and plan for and manage final physical database rollout.

3.3 Summary of differences between 3G and Relational Development environments: Let us summarise the specific differences between these two development environments. "Manual" means it must be coded, "Built in" means it is part of Oracle, "Constraint" means it is part of a database validation constraint, "DB Trigger" means it can be coded in SQL and encapsulated in the database. When we refer to a 3G, we are referring to a Third generation language such as C or COBOL using flat file storage:

- **Data Read Consistency, Table and Record Locking**: Manual in 3G - Built in, in Oracle
- **Table, Row, Column level security by user/role:** Manual in 3G - Built in, in Oracle
- **Functional security by table/user/role**: Manual in 3G - Built in, in Oracle
- **Primary Key allocation:** Manual in 3G - In Database in Oracle
- **Primary Key validation:** Manual in 3G - Constraint in Oracle
- **Unique Key validation**: Manual in 3G - Constraint in Oracle
- **Foreign Key validation:** Manual in 3G - Constraint in Oracle
- **NULL validation**: Manual in 3G - Constraint in Oracle
- **Cross data check validation:** Manual in 3G - Constraint in Oracle
- **Cascade UPDATE to other table(s):** Manual in 3G - DB Trigger in Oracle
- **Cascade DELETE to other table(s):** Manual in 3G - DB Trigger in Oracle
- **By-pass validation rules**: Possible in 3G - Impossible in Oracle
- **Performance risks of code**: Lower in 3G - Higher in Oracle
- **Need to understand Data structures**: Low in 3G - High in Oracle
- **Database design effort**: Low in 3G - High in Oracle
- **Coding design effort**: High in 3G - Low in Oracle
- **Unit and System testing design difficulty**: Difficult in 3G More predictable in Oracle database systems.

---o0o---

4. Basic Descriptions of Oracle products.

Here we present a short list of the main Oracle products as of version Oracle 9i, 10g and 11g. We include a short description of what these products are used for and the latest versions:

4.1 Core DBMS Products:

- **Oracle Database:** Versions 5, 6, 7, 8i, 9i, 10g, 11g: An object-relational database management system.

- **Enterprise Manager:** All DB versions: Oracle Enterprise Manager is used to configure and manage Oracle databases. Useful for: Change Management, Performance & Tuning, Diagnostics and Configuration Management.

4.2 Oracle Apps - E-Business Suite: v11, v12:

- **Oracle Applications** comprise the applications software or business software of Oracle. The term refers to the non-database and non-middleware parts of Oracle's application software range. Oracle sells many functional modules which use the Oracle DB as a back-end, notably:

- **Oracle Financials, Oracle HRMS, Oracle Projects, Oracle CRM, Oracle Procurement**, etc. The offering as of 2009 extends to supply-chain management, human-resource management, warehouse-management, customer-relationship management, call-center services, product-lifecycle management, and many other areas. Customers buy the basic modules and then tailor them to fit their own precise business model.

4.3 Development Tools - Data warehouse

- **Data Miner v10.1, 11.1:** Data Miner is the graphical user interface that helps data analysts mine their Oracle data to find valuable hidden information, and patterns.

- **Warehouse Builder, v11.2:** Oracle Warehouse Builder (OWB) is an ETL tool produced by Oracle that offers a graphical environment to build, manage and maintain data integration processes in business intelligence systems.

4.4 Development Tools - (General)

- **PL/SQL All DB versions:** PL/SQL is Oracle Corporation's proprietary procedural extension to SQL. PL/SQL code is stored and executed from within the database and can execute autonomously as a result of a database event (like an UPDATE). PL/SQL is central to most Oracle developments.

- **SQL*Plus and Worksheet All DB versions**: SQL*Plus is the most basic command line SQL interface where SQL can be entered and executed against a particular database schema. Worksheet provides a friendlier user interface to SQL.

- **SQL Developer 3.x:** SQL Developer is an integrated development environment for working with SQL and a number of Oracle databases. The product is part of all Oracle installations and bears some similarities to Toad. It allows data modelling, coding, database design oversight and editing and code debugging.

- **Oracle Designer: CASE, 2000, 6i, 9i, 10g:** Oracle Designer is Oracle's CASE tool for designing a complete database and application and generating both database and software objects into a physical database. Designer works standalone, or together with the Oracle Developer products. The future of Oracle Designer is uncertain, but it is still one of the most important and useful tools for the Oracle development professional. Designer provides very useful and resilient tools for complete design-to-build; from E-R modelling right through to complete physical database build in a target Oracle instance.

- **Developer suite, 5, 6i, 9i, 10g:** Oracle Developer Suite is a suite of development tools. The principal components were initially Oracle Forms and Oracle Reports, although the suite was later expanded to include JDeveloper.

- **JDeveloper, 9i, 10g:** JDeveloper is a freeware development environment supplied by Oracle. It offers features for development in Java, XML, SQL and PL/SQL, HTML, JavaScript, BPEL and PHP. JDeveloper covers the full development lifecycle from design through coding, debugging, optimization and profiling to deploying.

- **Application Express aka APEX, v1.5 to 4.2:** Oracle Application Express (Oracle APEX, previously named Oracle HTML DB) is a software development environment based on the Oracle database. It allows a fast development cycle to be achieved to create web based applications. It is easily up-scaleable to handle thousands of users.

---oOo---

5. The Oracle database architecture.

Oracle as a database is a highly evolved and complex environment. Here we will introduce you to some of the concepts which make up the basic Oracle database architecture. It is by no means comprehensive, but will give the reader an idea of how the database actually operates and where data is stored and processed.

5.1 Physical and logical structures

An Oracle database system comprises at least one "instance" of the Oracle database application, along with data storage associated with the database. An "instance" is a set of operating-system processes and memory-structures that interact with the database storage:

- **Oracle Processes:** Each "instance" has the same basic set of Oracle database processes. For example there is a process called PMON (the process monitor process) and SMON (the system monitor process).

- **Oracle Memory Area:** An Oracle instance shares some pre-allocated part of the memory of the server. The memory-structures of an Oracle server are referred to as the SGA (System Global Area). The SGA holds cache information about the Oracle instance, such as data-buffers, SQL commands, and user information.

- **Oracle Storage Infrastructure:** In addition to storage, the database consists of online redo logs, which hold transactional history. Processes can in turn archive the online redo logs into archive logs (offline redo logs), which provide the basis (if necessary) for data recovery and for the physical-standby forms of data replication using Oracle Data Guard.

- **Oracle RAC Options:** If the Oracle database administrator has implemented Oracle RAC (Real Application Clusters), then multiple instances, usually on different servers, attach to a central storage array. This scenario offers advantages such as better performance, scalability and redundancy. However, support becomes more complex, and many sites do not use RAC.

- **Oracle Grid Options:** In version 10*g*, grid computing introduced shared resources, where an instance can use CPU resources from another computer (node) in the grid.

- **Oracle Stored executables:** The Oracle DBMS can store and execute stored procedures and functions within itself using PL/SQL or Java.

5.2 Oracle Storage overview:

- **Logical Storage and Physical Storage:** The Oracle RDBMS stores data logically in the form of tablespaces and physically in the form of data files ("datafiles"). Tablespaces can contain various types of memory segments, such as Data Segments (tables), Index Segments (indexes on tables), etc. Segments in turn comprise one or more extents. Extents comprise groups of contiguous data blocks. Data blocks form the basic units of data storage. DBAs administer both logical and physical space allocations to database objects such as tables and indexes.

- **Table Partitions:** Oracle also includes a partitioning feature which is useful for dividing up very large tables. Partitioning allows the division of tables based on different sets of keys, determined by the database designer. For example, sales data may be partitioned by month because the sales data set may be huge. Dividing large data sets into monthly partitions makes them more manageable and their data more accessible. For example, specific partitions can then be easily added or dropped to help manage very large data sets.

- **SYSTEM tablespace:** One of the tablespaces in Oracle is somewhat special. This is the SYSTEM tablespace. Oracle database management tracks its data storage with the help of information stored in the SYSTEM tablespace. The SYSTEM tablespace contains the data dictionary. The data dictionary consists of a collection of tables that contains all the information about all user-objects in the database. So, for example, when a table is created by a designer, its definition is contained within the data dictionary in a group of "dictionary tables" which define the user table.

5.3 Oracle Disk files: At the physical level, data files comprise one or more data blocks, where the block size can vary between data files. Data files can occupy pre-allocated space in the file system of a computer server, utilize raw disk directly, or exist within ASM logical volumes.

Disk files primarily consist of the following types:

- **Data and index files:** These files are part of the physical storage of the database itself. They consist of the data dictionary data, user data, and index data. These files can be managed manually or managed by Oracle itself depending on configuration.

- **Redo log** files consist of all changes made to the database. They are most often used to recover from an instance failure. These files are stored multiple times, for extra security in case of disk failure.

- **Undo files:** These are special datafiles, which only contain transaction "undo" information. Undo information refers to the state of a table before a transaction started. These files are used to restore data after a ROLLBACK to maintain read consistency.

- **Archive log files:** These files are copies of the redo log files, but are usually stored at a different location. They are necessary, for example, to be applied to a standby database, or to perform recovery after a media failure.

- **TEMP files:** These are special datafiles used exclusively for temporary storage of data. They are often used for sorting operations of very large tables or global temporary tables.

- **Control file:** This is necessary for database start-up. The control file is a binary file that contains a record of the physical structure of a database and contains the names and locations of redo log files, the time stamp of the database creation, the current log file sequence number, checkpoint information, and so on.

5.4 Database Schema: A schema is a way of describing how a database is built or will be built. It comprises a collection of "schema objects". Examples of schema objects include: tables, views, sequences, synonyms, indexes, clusters, database links, snapshots, procedures, functions, packages. A schema always has a schema "owner", the Oracle user that owns the schema objects. This user has an Oracle user id and the privileges to create schema objects. In a development, it is generally a virtual "application owner" managed by the development DBA. Any Oracle user can potentially create schema objects that they own.

Default schemas in Oracle: Most Oracle database installations traditionally came with a default schema called SCOTT. After the installation process has set up the sample tables, the user can log into the database with the username SCOTT, password TIGER. The name of the SCOTT schema originated with Bruce Scott, one of the first employees at Oracle (then SDL), who had a cat named Tiger.

Oracle Corporation has de-emphasized the use of the SCOTT schema, as it uses few of the features of the more recent releases of Oracle. Most recent examples supplied by Oracle Corporation reference the default HR or OE schemas.

Other default schemas include:

- **SYS** (essential core database structures and utilities)

- **SYSTEM** (additional core database structures and utilities, and privileged account)

- **OUTLN** (utilized to store metadata for stored outlines for stable query-optimizer execution plans.

- **BI, IX, HR, OE, PM, and SH** (expanded sample schemas containing more data and structures than the older SCOTT schema).

5.5 Oracle Memory - The System Global Area (SGA)

Each Oracle instance uses a System Global Area or SGA- a shared-memory area - to store its data and control-information.

Each Oracle instance allocates itself an SGA when it starts and de-allocates it at shut-down time. The information in the SGA consists of the following elements, each of which has a fixed size, established at instance start-up. When an Oracle instance is started using Enterprise Manager or SQL*Plus, the amount of memory allocated for the SGA is displayed.

- **Redo log buffer:** this stores redo entries—a log of changes made to the database. The instance writes redo log buffers to the redo log as quickly and efficiently as possible. The redo log aids in instance recovery in the event of a system failure.

- **Shared pool:** this area of the SGA stores shared-memory structures such as shared SQL areas in the library cache and internal information in the data dictionary. An insufficient amount of memory allocated to the shared pool can cause performance degradation.

- **Large pool:** Optional area that provides large memory allocations for certain large processes, such as Oracle backup and recovery operations, and I/O server processes.

- **Database buffer cache:** Caches blocks of data retrieved from the database.

41

- **KEEP buffer pool:** A specialized type of database buffer cache that is tuned to retain blocks of data in memory for long periods of time.

- **RECYCLE buffer pool:** A specialized type of database buffer cache that is tuned to recycle or remove block from memory quickly.

- **nK buffer cache:** One of several specialized database buffer caches designed to hold block sizes different than the default database block size.

- **Java pool:** Used for all session-specific Java code and data in the Java Virtual Machine (JVM).

- **Streams pool:** Used by Oracle Streams to store information required by capture and apply.

5.5.1 Library cache helps speed up SQL execution: The library cache stores SQL which can be shared by multiple processes. The library cache stores the parse tree and the execution plan for every unique SQL statement. If multiple applications issue the same SQL statement, each application can access the shared SQL area. This reduces the amount of memory needed and reduces the processing-time used for parsing and execution planning.

5.5.2 Data dictionary cache: The data dictionary comprises a set of tables and views that map the structure of the database. Oracle databases store information here about the logical and physical structure of the database. The data dictionary contains information such as:

- **User information**, such as user privileges.

- **Integrity constraints** defined for tables in the database.

- **Names and data types** of all columns in database tables.

- **Information on space** allocated and used for schema objects.

An Oracle instance frequently accesses the data dictionary in order to parse SQL statements. The operation of Oracle depends on ready access to the data dictionary, because performance bottlenecks in the data dictionary affect Oracle users. Because of this, DBAs ensure that the data dictionary cache has sufficient capacity to cache this data. Without enough memory for the data-dictionary cache, users may experience performance degradation, so allocating sufficient memory to the shared pool where the data dictionary cache resides, avoids these particular performance problems.

5.6 Program Global Area

The Program Global Area or PGA memory-area of an Oracle instance contains data and control-information for Oracle's server-processes.

The size and content of the PGA depends on the Oracle-server options installed. This area consists of the following components:

- **Stack-space:** the memory that holds the session's variables, arrays, and so on.

- **Session-information:** unless using the multithreaded server, the instance stores its session-information in the PGA. (In a multithreaded server, the session-information goes in the SGA.)

- **Private SQL-area:** an area which holds information such as bind-variables and runtime-buffers.

- **Sorting area:** an area in the PGA which holds information on sorts, hash-joins, etc.

5.7 Dynamic performance views

The dynamic performance views (also known as "fixed views") within an Oracle database present information from virtual tables (X\$ tables) built on the basis of database memory. Database users can access the V\$ views (named after the prefix of their synonyms) to obtain information on database structures and performance.

5.8 Process architectures in Oracle: The Oracle RDBMS relies on a group of processes running simultaneously in the background and interacting to monitor and expedite database operations. Here are some of the main processes and a brief description of what they do, to give an idea of the background processing in an Oracle instance:

- Advanced queuing processes (Qnnn)

- Archiver processes (ARCn)

- Checkpoint process (CKPT) *REQUIRED*

- Coordinator-of-job-queues process (CJQn): dynamically spawns slave processes for job-queues

- Database writer processes (DBWn) *REQUIRED*

- Dispatcher processes (Dnnn): multiplex server-processes on behalf of users

- Main Data Guard Broker monitor process (DMON)

- Job-queue slave processes (Jnnn)

- Log-writer process (LGWR) *REQUIRED*

- Log-write network-server (LNSn): transmits redo logs in Data Guard environments

- Logical standby coordinator process (LSP0): controls Data Guard log-application

- Media-recovery process (MRP): detached recovery-server process

- Memory-manager process (MMAN): used for internal database tasks such as Automatic Shared Memory Management

- Memory-monitor process (MMON): process for automatic problem-detection, self-tuning and statistics-gathering

- Memory-monitor light process (MMNL): gathers and stores Automatic Workload Repository (AWR) data

- mmon slaves (Mnnnn—M0000, M0001, etc.): background slaves of the MMON process

- Process-monitor process (PMON) *REQUIRED*

- Process spawner (PSP0): spawns Oracle processes

- Queue-monitor coordinator process (QMNC): dynamically spawns queue monitor slaves

- Queue-monitor processes (QMNn)

- Recoverer process (RECO)

- Remote file-server process (RFS)

- Shared server processes (Snnn): serve client-requests

- System monitor process (SMON)

5.9 User processes, connections and sessions

Oracle Database terminology uses the following terms in describing how end-users interact with the database:

- **User processes** involve the invocation of application software.

- **Connections** refer to the pathways linking a user process to an Oracle instance. A user or process is said to "connect" to an Oracle instance.

- **Sessions** consist of specific connections to an Oracle instance. Each session within an instance has a session identifier or "SID" (not to be confused with an Oracle instance System Id).

5.10 Concurrency and locking

Oracle databases control simultaneous access to data resources with locks.

5.11 Configuration - The PFILE

Database administrators control many of the database "tuneable" variations in an Oracle instance by means of values in a parameter file - the PFILE. This file in its ASCII default form ("pfile") normally has a name of the format init<SID-name>.ora.

5.12 Internationalisation

Oracle Database software comes in 63 language-versions (including regional variations such as British English and American English). Variations between versions cover the names of days and months, abbreviations, time-symbols such as A.M. and A.D., and sorting.

---oOo---

6. Tools: Oracle's own Design / Development tools.

6.1 Introduction: There is a wide range of possible routes to designing and developing an Oracle application, depending on the type of system. It may be OLAP or OLTP. It may be a mainly batch processing system or a predominantly online system. Obviously a data warehousing application design, demanding high performance query processing would not be undertaken in the same way as an OLTP application which is heavily biased towards online data entry processing. The priorities are different and the design approach and tools are also different.

Oracle provides its own design and development toolsets to provide for the full life-cycle of a development from User Requirements, through logical and physical design to change management of finished software.

6.2 Oracle Designer: Oracle Designer is the primary CASE tool provided by Oracle and is a mature product. It provides a comprehensive range of logical and physical design facilities which include the creation of the scripts to actually build the physical database at a target location. Here is a summary of the facilities provided by Oracle Designer 10g:

Business Process Modelling

- Process Modeller

Systems Analysis Modelling

- E-R Diagrammer
- Dataflow
- Function Hierarchy

Design Wizards

- Database Wizard
- Application Wizard
- Reverse engineer database to Schema model

Systems Design

- Data Schema
- Module Logic
- Module Data
- Preferences
- Module Structure

Client/Server Generators

- Server
- Forms
- Reports
- Graphics
- Visual Basic
- Web server
- Microsoft Help
- C++ Object Layer

Utilities

- Repository Object Navigator
- Matrix
- Repository Reports
- Admin Utility
- SQL*Plus

The Future of Oracle Designer: There is some ambiguity about the future of the Designer product. No new release was made for Oracle 11g. However, the product is still actively supported by Oracle. At the time of writing there is no alternative, fully integrated Oracle-built CASE design product in sight. So, Oracle Designer still provides an outstanding spread of modelling facilities and database integration.

Learning Oracle Designer: Designer is a very large product and has 15 years of evolutionary background in Oracle, during which the product has developed into a highly sophisticated tool. Therefore, it is not a software product that the average designer or database developer is going to learn in an afternoon - it requires an investment in time.

However, because it is entirely modular, a designer may use only those components they wish to use. Many aspects of Oracle Designer are unnecessary for many types of application. Therefore, the problem of learning to use the product is limited to what you choose to use it for. There is a wealth of training documentation and video presentations available to help a new user to learn to use Oracle Designer.

Why we suggest you use Oracle Designer: We have chosen to use Oracle Designer as the main Design Tool and methodology in the other volumes of these guides. We think we have a good reason for this: Designer is a mature, stable product and comes directly from Oracle. At the time of writing there is no other integrated Oracle CASE tool. Designer tends to impose a discipline on the analyst-designer which we find important - since early design errors tend to create large rework efforts later. Oracle Designer works well in a multi-user environment, can handle simultaneous multi-application designs and it integrates especially well in a RAD design methodology (which we also favour). Having said all this, no doubt an alternative CASE product will eventually supersede Designer 10g and we are constantly evaluating new products both from Oracle and 3rd party vendors.

How to start using Oracle Designer: Once installed, it is possible for an analyst-designer to start using Oracle Designer at either a logical or physical level. This means that it isn't necessary to pass through all the analytical stages before getting down to the main physical database design process. So a design user can choose to skip the "Model System Requirements" facilities and go straight to the physical design level using the "Design Editor". This means that it isn't essential to create an Entity-Relationship model first before defining the physical database schema model. Very often, this is the most obvious route and saves time. This is especially true where the schema model is pretty self-evident to the designer.

Integrating Designer in a RAD process: Designer works well in a RAD environment because an experienced designer can define a database prototype very quickly, using the Designer Editor and present it to a user group. Even better, in the case of an OLTP system, Designer allows for the creation of fast prototype front end forms and reports, which can also be used by a user group to get a feel for the implications of their design decisions (issues such as data validation for example often only emerge when a user actually starts to use a physical interface). So regardless of the final build interface, Designer can be extremely useful in creating and refining a database design with recursive prototyping. User refinements are fast and easy to implement

48

and regenerate into a physical prototype database for re-presentation to the user group. All the Design Team leader must do is maintain a control on the User-Designer sessions, properly document the incremental changes, ensure that they are normalised, that they are properly implemented in Designer and finally, that they are correctly generated into the physical database. After a number of these design iterations, the database design will begin to stabilise. Finally, the last iteration from Designer will, indeed, be the final normalized model.

6.3 SQL Developer: SQL Developer is an integrated development environment for working with SQL in Oracle databases. Oracle provides this product free. SQL Developer offers end-to-end development of PL/SQL applications, a worksheet for running queries and scripts, a DBA console for managing the database, a reports interface, a data modelling interface with a migration platform for moving 3rd party databases to Oracle.

SQL Developer is not a CASE tool and it's no substitute for Oracle Designer, but it does have some overlapping features which are useful when managing a physical database design. Some small applications can be adequately managed using SQL Developer. It is especially useful when debugging PL/SQL procedures and triggers because it provides instant compilation and error information about a piece of PL/SQL code. It also provides a nice multi-database overview. And it can also be used for MySQL and other databases as well as Oracle databases. This can be useful: SQL Developer is gradually becoming a competitor for TOAD, the 3rd party DB management tool.

6.4 Oracle Warehouse Builder (OWB): Oracle Warehouse Builder (OWB) is an ETL tool that offers a graphical environment to build, manage and maintain data integration processes in business intelligence systems. The primary use for OWB is consolidation of heterogeneous data sources in data warehousing and data migration from legacy systems, including Oracle systems. It offers capabilities for relational, dimensional and metadata data modelling, data profiling, data cleansing and data auditing. OWB only supports a single target database - Oracle (and flat files) but no other proprietary database targets.

OWB consists of two main components:

- The design environment, which is concerned with working with Meta data (abstract representations of warehouse objects, together with business rules).

- The runtime environment, which takes this metadata and turns it into physical database objects and process flows.

In Oracle 11g, OWB uses a separate database schema for storing OWB data. OWB users work in a workspace as opposed to having their own repository schemas as found in Oracle10g. All of the workspaces are owned by the OWBSYS account and are managed or stored within OWBSYS schema. This greatly simplifies management of OWB objects within the database. Users within the database can be added as OWB users via the granted role of OWB_USER.

The GUI interface provides an easy to use method of defining source databases such as DB2, DRDA, Informix, SQL Server, Sybase, and Teradata. Other accessible sources include any data store accessible through the ODBC Data Source Administrator, including Excel and MS Access. In addition, the GUI allows the designer-user to define Source-Target mappings, transformation definitions, and ETL process flows.

6.5 Oracle SQL Developer Data Modeller: We make special mention of this product because it is one of the few possible Database design tools which Oracle provides as an alternative to the traditional Oracle Designer product.

The Data Modeller product is free and can be installed as a stand alone client or together with Oracle SQL Developer. Using Oracle SQL Developer Data Modeller, users can connect to Oracle Databases 9.2.0.1 and above, Oracle Database 10g and Oracle Database 11g. There is also support for IBM DB2 LUW V7 and V8, IBM DB2/390, Microsoft SQL Server 2000 and 2005 or a standard ODBC/JDBC driver for selective import of database objects.

Oracle SQL Developer Data Modeller has a number of interrelated modelling techniques. The main central diagram is the logical model for creating Entity Relationship Diagrams (ERD), using either the Barker or Bachman notations, or partial support for Information Engineering. Linked to the logical model is the multi-dimensional model, used to model star schemas (facts, dimensions and levels). The datatypes model allows users to model structured types (SQL99), which can be used in the logical or relational models as data types.

The relational model, supporting tables, columns and relationships, can be built from scratch or forward-engineered from the logical model. Users can build one or more synchronized relational models from the central logical model. In turn, each relational model supports one or more physical models. The advantage is that developers can generate different database or platform specific DDL scripts, depending on the physical model selected. The physical model supports specific data constructs in Oracle databases, IBM DB2 and Microsoft SQL Server.

The Data modeller is a useful and fairly easy tool to learn and use. It is similar in some respects to parts of the TOAD and ERWIN products. It isn't as complete and fully integrated as Oracle Designer, but it may well be a useful alternative to Oracle Designer in some types of development. The tool provides a useful Import-Export utility to move designs between itself and Oracle Designer and has a well-featured configuration control system embedded into the product.

6.6 Oracle Enterprise Manager: We will cover this very sophisticated database management product in a later volume; however, we wanted to provide an overview now, because it is such an important component in a typical Oracle Development.

Enterprise Manager (from 10 onwards) is a web-based Oracle database management utility. Prior to that, the product was a Java based consol and probably one of Oracle's best known products. The product continues to develop with new Oracle versions, but its core functionality remains the management of the Oracle Database.

Here are some of the main features of Enterprise Manager:

- **Instance Admin:** Allows admin of multiple Oracle instances - start up-shutdown etc.

- **Security:** Oracle User, Role, Privilege Administration.

- **Schema Admin:** Oracle Schema Administration (tables, indexes etc).

- **Storage - Logical and Physical Storage Admin:** Oracle Storage Administration (Tablespaces, Datafiles, Rollback segments).

- **Distributed database Admin:** Links, Streams, Data Replication.

- **Data warehouse admin:** OLAP management.

- **Backup Management:** Including Data Management (Analyze object etc.).

- **Performance and Resource use Management**

---o0o---

7. Implementing Oracle DB and Oracle tools - Overview.

This is an enormous subject to cover in detail and the installation issues for Oracle databases depend entirely on the target environment, the use of the database and the physical configuration of the server hardware.

However, here we will explain some general principles about how Oracle is installed and how it works together with other product components. We will do this by describing a simple basic Oracle installation.

- **The Database installation:** The Oracle database comes with a set of installation software which will allow a system administrator to build an Oracle instance and a basic Oracle database on a target filesystem (UNIX) or drive and directory (Windows). The installation software will only prompt for the SYSTEM and SYS user passwords, some file location information and a name for the Oracle database.

- **Basic Configuration:** After a basic instance and database have been created, a DBA will test that the database is functional and can be used by other users. At this point, an experienced DBA will carry out some initial configuration of the database to ensure that it has sufficient memory allocations (SGA etc.) for its intended purposes. Issues such as database BACKUP will also be implemented at this stage before the database becomes accessible to the users.

- **SQL*Plus command line consol:** Some basic tools are installed by the database installer. These will include SQL*Plus. This allows the DBA to carry out command line instructions for starting, stopping, mounting, dismounting, opening and closing the database.

- **Enterprise Manager:** The most important additional tool (which) the DBA will require is Enterprise Manager. This provides graphic detail of various components of the database operation. Again, an experienced DBA will probably use their own diagnostic scripts to understand and alter a database configuration, but Enterprise Manager does provide a simple to use interface. Enterprise Manager uses a web-based interface (since Oracle v10g) and this means that Oracle's HTTP server must also be installed. This is basically just a version of the Apache web server. Its configuration is well documented.

- **TNSNAMES.ora:** This is an important file that all client users of the Oracle database must have. It contains the essential connection information for client software to connect to one or more Oracle database instances. Here is an extract from a typical TNSNAMES.ora, defining a database instance called TRACK on a host server also called TRACK:

```
TRACK =
    (DESCRIPTION =
        (ADDRESS = (PROTOCOL = TCP)(HOST =
        track)(PORT = 1521))
        (CONNECT_DATA =
        (SERVER = DEDICATED)
        (SERVICE_NAME = track)
        )
    )
```

Advice: Most client connection problems result from problems with local TNSNAME.ora file definitions.

Tools installation:

- **SQL Developer** is installed as a client on each user's client PC.

- **Oracle Designer:** Designer is a multi-user client server application. The design is stored in a design repository (which is just a shared database schema). This is installed on a server in a pre-defined Oracle database (but normally kept separate from the development database used to build the physical application database itself). Oracle Designer users need to have a client installation on their PCs and a valid copy of the appropriate TNSNAMES.ora file with the connection definition of the Designer repository, the application development databases and any test databases they are going to use.

- **SQL*Plus** for development is installed as a client on each designer-developer's PC.

- **Oracle Developer Suite (apart from Designer):** If the application development requires these tools, they also need to be installed as clients on designer-developer's PCs. Forms and Reports 10g Builders have client-server development implementations, even though generated Oracle Forms run in a Java EE environment.

Generated reports run using the Oracle Application Server Reports Service.

---oOo---

8. Various 3rd Party Tools: A Quick review.

8.1 Introduction: Quite a variety of third party tools have built up around Oracle over the years. Some are good products and some are quite mediocre. We tend to favour using Oracle "native" products, because they are generally available on all sites and are consistent with the installed database versions. However, this is not always true.I have encountered sites which refuse to pay the small extra licence fees to install Oracle Designer and insist on using 3rd party tools. So it's difficult to be dogmatic about what is best. In general, we favour using Oracle Tools to manage Oracle designs, but if they are not available, it is possible to manage quite well with some decent 3rd party tools. Let us take a look at the "best of the crop":

8.2 TOAD: **T**ool for **O**racle **A**pplication **D**evelopers (TOAD) is a software application from Quest Software, used for development and administration of various relational databases using SQL. Toad supports a lot of different databases and this is useful in some environments. It's easy to use and has some excellent PL/SQL debugging features (similar to SQL Developer) and provides some useful performance tuning facilities. It is not free. Recommended by multi-database-provider environments where databases from several suppliers are running side by side and interacting.

8.3 Erwin Data Modeller: This is a tool for data modelling (data requirements analysis, database design etc.) of custom developed information systems, including databases of transactional systems and data marts. Erwin's data modelling engine is based upon the IDEF1X method, although it now supports diagrams displayed with information engineering notation as well. Erwin has the following basic features:

- Logical Data Modelling: Purely logical models may be created, from which physical models may be derived.

- Physical Data Modelling: Purely physical models may be created.

- Logical-to-Physical Transformation: Includes an abbreviation/naming dictionary called "Naming Standards Editor" and a logical-to-RDBMS data type mapping facility called "Datatype Standards Editor", both of which are customizable with entries and basic rule enforcement.

- Forward engineering: Once the database designer is satisfied with the physical model, the tool can automatically generate a SQL DDL (data definition language) script that can either be directly executed in the RDBMS environment or saved to a file.

- Reverse engineering: If an analyst needs to examine and understand an existing data structure, Erwin will depict the physical database objects in an Erwin model file.

- Model-to-model comparison: The "Complete/Compare" facility allows an analyst or designer to view the differences between two model files (including real-time reverse-engineered files for instance) to understand changes between two versions of a model.

8.4 Informatica Power Centre: This is a product which is quite similar to Oracle Warehouse Builder (OWB) and provides many of the same facilities. It consists of a number of components to allow a data warehouse designer model an ETL process and generate Extract, Transform and Load code.

---oOo---

9. Glossary of Terms.

3G language: Most popular general-purpose languages today, such as C, C++, C#, Java, BASIC and Pascal, are also third-generation languages, although C++, Java and C# follow a completely different path as they are object-oriented in nature.

Third generation (3G) languages tend to focus on software structures and structured development. They have no connection with concepts of object encapsulation, including the idea that a database table may autonomously incorporate its own validation rules and may manifest and control its own behaviour under varying conditions such as a database transaction.

APEX: Apex is Oracle Application Express, an Oracle product that has been a long time in development and is the latest in a set of Oracle front-end design and development tools. APEX is embedded and integrated into the application database and provides a sophisticated toolkit for rapid web application development against an Oracle database. APEX is basically a web front end development environment based on an Oracle database. For an experienced developer it can be a very good tool to produce a resilient dynamic html web-based front-end. Despite the claims of Oracle, it is really *not* a development tool for a novice. However, it is an excellent product and has rapidly replaced Oracle Forms and Reports as the front-end of choice for many Oracle applications where a web interface is needed.

Commit: Committing a transaction means making permanent the changes performed by the SQL statements within the transaction. A transaction is a sequence of SQL statements. Commit overrides all previous save points in the transaction and releases all previous transaction locks. Oracle recommends that you explicitly end every transaction in your application programs with a COMMIT or ROLLBACK statement. If a transaction is not explicitly committed and a program terminates abnormally, then the last uncommitted transaction is automatically rolled back.

Constraints (database constraints): Constraints are rules of *data integrity* for a database that limit the acceptable data values for a table. They are the optional schema objects that depend on a table. The existence of a table without any constraint is possible, but the existence of a constraint without any table is not possible.

Constraints enforce business rules in a database. If a constraint is violated during a transaction, the transaction will fail, be rolled-back and a specific error occur.

Constraints can be created along with the table in the CREATE TABLE statement. Addition and deletion of constraints can be done in the ALTER TABLE statement. The following types of constraints are available in Oracle Database:

- **NOT NULL:** It enforces that a column, declared as not null, cannot have any NULL values. For example, if an employee's hire date is not known, then that employee may not be considered as a valid employee.

- **UNIQUE:** It ensures that columns protected by this constraint cannot have duplicate values.

- **PRIMARY KEY:** It is responsible for uniquely identifying a row in a table. A table can have only one PRIMARY KEY constraint. A PRIMARY KEY constraint completely includes both the NOT NULL and UNIQUE constraints. It is enforced with an index on all columns in the key.

- **FOREIGN KEY:** It is also known as referential integrity constraint. It enforces that values referenced in one table are defined in another table. It establishes a parent-child or reference-dependent relationship between the two tables.

- **CHECK:** It enforces that columns must meet a specific condition that is evaluated to a Boolean value. If the value evaluates to false, then the database will raise an exception, and not allow the INSERT and UPDATE statements to operate on columns.

Data Consistency and Concurrency: In a single-user database, a user can modify data without concern for other users modifying the same data at the same time. However, in a multi-user database, statements within multiple simultaneous transactions can update the same data. Transactions executing simultaneously must produce meaningful and consistent results. Therefore, a multi-user database must provide the following conditions:

- Data concurrency, which ensures that users can access data at the same time.

- Data consistency, which ensures that each user sees a consistent view of the data, including visible changes made by the user's own transactions and committed transactions of other users.

To describe consistent transaction behaviour when transactions run concurrently, database researchers defined a "transaction isolation" model called serializability. A serializable transaction operates in an environment that makes it appear as if no other users were modifying data in the database.

While this isolation between transactions is generally desirable, running many applications in serializable mode can seriously compromise application throughput. Complete isolation of concurrently running transactions could mean that one transaction cannot perform an insertion into a table being queried by another transaction. So, basically, real world considerations require a compromise between perfect transaction isolation and performance. Oracle maintains data consistency by using a so-called multi-version consistency model and various types of locks and transactions. In this way, the database can present a view of data to multiple concurrent users, with each view consistent to a point in time. Because different versions of data blocks can exist simultaneously, transactions can read the version of data committed at the point in time required by a query and return results that are consistent to a single point in time.

This complex infrastructure is built into Oracle Transaction Processing (TP) and developers need not concern themselves with it - it works very effectively.

Data dictionary: Oracle's data dictionary provides information that Oracle needs in order to perform its tasks. This information consists of definitions, storage size for database objects (tables, views, indexes etc. etc.), default column values, integrity constraints, names of and privileges granted to users, auditing information and more. The data dictionary is stored in a group of tables owned by SYS (the so called dictionary base tables). Their content is available through static dictionary "views". These views and tables should not be written to, only selected. The base tables are stored in the SYSTEM tablespace - which is always available when the Oracle database is open.

DBA: A Database Administrator: This is the person (database "role") responsible for the installation, configuration, upgrade, administration, monitoring and maintenance of (Oracle) databases within an organisation or in a development project. The role includes the design and development of database strategies, database monitoring, database performance tuning and capacity planning for future expansion. A DBA is also responsible for the planning, co-ordination and implementation of security measures to safeguard controlled access to the database, database availability and database backup and failure management.

Edgar Codd (1923 - 2003) was an English computer scientist who, while working for IBM, invented the relational model for database management, the theoretical basis for relational databases. The relational model, a very influential general theory of data management, remains his most important achievement.

ETL - Extract - Transform - Load: In data exploitation, Extract, Transform and Load (ETL) refers to a process in database usage and especially in data warehousing that involves:

- Extracting data from outside sources,

- Transforming it to fit operational needs such as complex reporting or data mining,

- Loading it into an end target database which may be an operational data store, data mart or data warehouse where it becomes useable for other reporting or data mining purposes.

FIFO (as in locking): If multiple users require a lock on a row or rows in a table, the first user to request the lock obtains it, and the remaining users are enqueued using a first-in, first-out (FIFO) method. This means the first lock requester gets the lock first, and so on.

Flat file structures: A flat file database is a very primitive data store, using a plain text file. Each line of the text file holds one record, with fields separated by delimiters, such as commas or tabs. Software reads and writes to flat files very efficiently, but managing issues such as data integrity must be manually coded into the software, using these flat structures. Flat file storage has generally been superseded by the use of various structured database storage methods.

Grid Computing: Grid computing is the joining together of computer resources from multiple locations to achieve a common objective. What distinguishes grid computing from systems such as cluster computing is that grids tend to be more loosely coupled, heterogeneous, and geographically dispersed. Although a single grid can be dedicated to a particular application, commonly a grid is used for a variety of purposes. Oracle's Grid computing enables the creation of a single IT infrastructure that can be shared by multiple business processes. Oracle

Enterprise Manager is used to define and configure dispersed Oracle grid resources.

Hot backups: Normal system backups, referred to as either Hot or Cold backups, are used to protect from media failure. A Cold backup, that is, one done with the database in a shutdown state, provides a complete copy of the database which can be restored exactly.

A Hot backup - or one taken while the database is active - can only give a read consistent copy, but doesn't handle active transactions. All data in the Oracle or system buffers and all non-committed changes may be lost, unless a redo log switch is forced, the resulting archive log and a control file copy taken along with the hot file backup. In order to use the hot backup methodology, the database must be in archivelog mode.

Denormalization: This is the process of grouping data from several related tables into a single "denormalized" table. In some cases, denormalization is a means of addressing query performance. OLAP type applications often denormalize data to achieve complex queries with reasonable response times. A normalized design will store different, but related, pieces of information in separate logical tables which are, therefore, related. Completing a database query that draws information from several tables (using a join operation) can be slow. If many relations are joined, it may be unusable in an OLAP application and denormalization may be the only solution.

DDL: Data Definition Language: Data definition language syntax is used to define data structures, especially database schemas. Examples of DDL include object creation statements such as:

    "CREATE TABLE INVOICE_HEADERS......."

DML: Data Manipulation Language: This is a family of syntax elements in SQL which are used for inserting, updating and deleting data in a database. Read-only queries of data, (select, in SQL) are also considered a component of DML. Examples of DML include select statements such as:

    SELECT * FROM INVOICE_LINES

    WHERE INVOICE_NO = '7627682'...

Index: An Index is an Oracle database object associated with a table. Indexes provide improved access to table rows by storing sorted values from specific columns and using those sorted values to find associated table rows more easily.

This means that data can be found without having to look at more than a fraction of the total rows within a table. Indexes are optional, but generally associated with primary and unique keys and often with foreign key columns. The use of indexes is not always positive. An index may improve data retrieval speed, but inserting data is less efficient, because every new record means that one or more indexes needs to be updated. This reduces performance and this can be a disadvantage for OLTP database processing. However, in a data warehouse environment (where transaction processing doesn't happen) indexes can be used without too much consideration and generally yield performance improvements.

Instance (Oracle instance): A database instance is a set of memory structures that manage database files. A database is a set of physical files on disk created by the "CREATE DATABASE" statement. The instance manages its associated data and serves the users of the database. Every running Oracle database is associated with at least one Oracle database instance.

Locking: In a multi-user system, many users may wish to update the same data at the same time. Locking allows only one user to update a particular data block, during which time another person cannot modify the same data. The basic idea of locking is that when a user modifies data through a transaction, that data is locked by that transaction until the transaction is committed or rolled back. The lock is held until the transaction is complete - this is known as data concurrency.

The second purpose of locking is to ensure that all processes have read access to the original data as they were at the time the query began (modification not yet committed). This is known as read consistency.

Although locks are vital to enforce database consistency, they can create performance problems. Every time one process issues a lock, another user may be shut out from updating/deleting the locked row or table. Oracle allows a user to lock whatever resources they need. This can be a single row, many rows, an entire table, and even many tables. But the larger the scope of the lock, the more processes are potentially shut out to processing by other users. Data however can always be viewed by other users in its pre-committed state.

Optimistic and pessimistic locking strategies in Oracle: This is most relevant to web-based TP systems. Normally Oracle resources such as rows or tables are locked automatically when certain DML commands are issued, such as INSERT, UPDATE, and DELETE. However, in stateless environments such as many html-based internet interfaces, it is often necessary to issue explicit locking commands in the database interface when selecting data to be presented to a web-based client. This can be done in two ways: by using an optimistic locking strategy or a pessimistic locking strategy.

- Pessimistic: The disadvantage of pessimistic locking is that a resource is locked from the time it is first accessed in a transaction until the transaction is finished, making it inaccessible to other transactions during that time.

- Optimistic: With optimistic locking, a resource is not actually locked when it is first accessed by a transaction. Instead of locking a record, with the optimistic locking strategy, the "state" of the data in the record at the time when it would have been locked (with the pessimistic locking approach) is saved. Other transactions are able to concurrently access the record. So, there is a possibility of conflicting changes. At commit time, when the resource is about to be updated in the database, the state of the resource is read again from the database and compared to the state that was saved when the resource was first accessed in the transaction. If the two states differ, thena conflicting update was made, and the transaction is rolled back. This is the least convenient and safe locking strategy but is often the only strategy available in internet based applications.

Maintenance backlogs - maintenance workload: Software maintenance backlogs and costs are a major component in long-term system costs and service levels. Software maintenance demands and costs can rapidly increase and become many times greater than an original software system investment, both in terms of cost and human resources.

This happens especially when there is a significant flux in system requirements or when the underlying system is very costly to alter. The latter problem tends to be the result of poor strategic and design decisions, permitting the incorporation of software or other structural dependencies. In effect, this means that a simple software maintenance issue in one part of a system may give rise to much wider impact analysis and change control implications elsewhere in one or more related systems. Maintenance backlogs rapidly develop and can hinder an IT department's ability to function in a normal operational sense.

Methodologies - project methodologies, software engineering techniques: A software development methodology is a framework used to structure, plan, and control the process of development of an information system. A methodology includes the definition of software deliverables that a project team will develop as part of a software application. There are many methodologies, for example Prototyping, Rapid Application Development, Waterfall methodology, Spiral Methodology, Incremental Methodology etc. In an Oracle environment, a RAD or Prototyping approach works best, in general. See RAD below.

OLAP: On-line Analytical Processing: This is a type or part of a system characterized by a relatively low volume of transactions. Queries are often very complex and involve aggregations. For OLAP systems a response time is a measure of effectiveness. OLAP applications are widely used by Data Mining techniques. In an OLAP database there is aggregated, historical data, stored in multi-dimensional schemas (usually star schema) which may be heavily denormalized.

OLTP: On-line Transaction processing: This is a type or part of a system which is characterized by a large number of short on-line transactions (INSERT, UPDATE, and DELETE). The main emphasis for OLTP systems is put on very fast query processing, maintaining data integrity in multi-access environments and an effectiveness measured by the number of transactions per second. OLTP is the "system opposite" of OLAP (On-line Analytical Processing), which is used to aggregate and obtain information rather than make user transactions.

Oracle Developer Suite: The latest release, Oracle Developer Suite 10g consists of the following components:

- **Oracle Forms:** Oracle Forms is a software product for creating screens that interact with an Oracle database. It has an IDE including an object navigator, property sheet and code editor that uses PL/SQL. It was originally developed to run server-side in character mode terminal sessions. It was ported to other platforms, including Windows, to function in a client-server environment. Later versions were ported to Java where it runs in a Java EE container and can integrate with Java and web services. The primary focus of Forms is to create data entry systems that access an Oracle database. Oracle Forms is integrated into Oracle Designer and Forms can be generated directly from the Module Design toolset.

- **Oracle Reports:** Oracle Reports is a tool for developing reports against data stored in an Oracle database. Oracle Reports consists of Oracle Reports Developer and Oracle Application Server Reports Services (a component of the Oracle Application Server). Oracle Reports is integrated into Oracle Designer and Reports can be generated directly from the Module Design toolset.

- **Oracle Designer:** Oracle's primary CASE tool (as of 10g). Useful for Analysis, Logical and Physical design, process modelling, schema modelling and functional and module design and build.

- **Oracle Discoverer:** Oracle Discoverer is a tool-set for ad-hoc querying, reporting, data analysis, and Web-publishing for the Oracle Database environment. Oracle Corporation markets it as a business intelligence product. It was originally a stand-alone product; however it has become a component of the Oracle Fusion Middleware suite, and renamed Oracle Business Intelligence Discoverer.

- **Oracle JDeveloper:** JDeveloper is a freeware IDE supplied by Oracle Corporation. It offers features for development in Java, XML, SQL and PL/SQL, HTML, JavaScript, BPEL and PHP. JDeveloper covers the full development lifecycle from design through to coding, debugging, optimization and profiling to deploying.

PL/SQL: Procedural Language / Structured Query Language (PL/SQL) is Oracle's procedural extension language for SQL and the Oracle database. SQL is limited by not having any procedure syntax. The concept of "if" simply doesn't exist in SQL. SQL is a set language and deals only with the basic transactional events of INSERT, UPDATE, and DELETE and of course the basic query syntax of SELECT.

Prior to PL/SQL, programmers were obliged to "wrap up" tracts of SQL in other 3G languages (which Oracle provided) such as Pro*C, Pro*Cobol, etc.Whilst this worked fine, Oracle needed a new procedural language which could be stored and executed from within the database itself and PL/SQL was therefore released with Oracle version 7. It has a full set of procedural syntax and is a relatively easy language to use. Needless to say the PL/SQL is very much biased towards database processing and has a limited amount of other non dataset I/O facilities.

Procedures and Triggers: PL/SQL program units can be stored as procedures and triggers in the database. This is a very useful way of controlling the behaviour of a table during a DML transaction. For example, imagine that an Order Header table also stores the total value for all its Order Lines as a denormalized column. When a new order line is added, this total most be recalculated and the Order Header table updated. The same is true when an Order line is deleted or updated. Again, the order header total value needs to be recalculated and the Order Header table kept up to date with the new total value.

- This scenario is ideally managed using 3 triggers on the Order Line table which will "fire" ON-INSERT, ON-UPDATE, and ON-DELETE.

- Each of these triggers then calls a stored PL/SQL procedure, called, for example, RECALCULATE_ORDER_TOTAL.

- This procedure will recalculate the sum of the ORDER_LINE_VALUE and then issue an UPDATE of the ORDER_HEADER table to update the stored total value.

Performance: Oracle performance is usually measured by processing cycle times, or data throughput rates. Oracle performance can be a critical issue in very large databases (VLDB), where mission critical tasks can be delayed by poor processing times. Also, performance is not a static issue. Performance may degrade over time as data volumes or number of user processes increase or as tables or indexes become more and more disorganised. Performance is generally affected by the following issues: Appropriate server sizing, considerate Oracle instance configuration, optimal physical database design (indexes, partitioning etc), SQL software design (optimal access path for retrieving data), and the quality and frequency of database maintenance.

Primary and unique keys - the differences: In logical database design, a normalised entity is allocated a Unique Identifier (UID). This UID consists of one or more attributes which, taken together, can be used to uniquely identify one instance of that entity (or one record in a table).

For example, in a Human Resources database this unique identifier might be Social Security Number or some artificial "surrogate" key created by the company, such as Employee Id. Very often an entity has more than one possible unique identifier. Name, date of birth and place of birth can perhaps be used as a unique id in some applications. During the transition from logical design to physical design, certain decisions need to be made about these identifiers. One of them must be selected as the Primary Key of the table, and the remaining alternative unique identifiers must be defined as unique keys. A primary key is the main method by which a record is identified. Unique keys are alternate methods of identifying a record. Both types of key MUST be unique, and the database will enforce this uniqueness using Primary and Unique Key Constraints, which basically enforce the uniqueness using Unique Indexes on the defined columns. It is therefore imperative to be absolutely sure about the definition of these keys during the Oracle database design phase.

Rapid Application Development (RAD): Rapid application development is a term originally used to describe a software development process introduced by James Martin, the Systems Design researcher, in 1991. RAD is a software development methodology, which involves iterative design and development and the construction of prototypes. The basic principles of RAD are:

- Key objective is for fast development and delivery of a high quality system with a relatively low investment.

- RAD aims to produce high quality systems quickly, primarily via iterative Prototyping, active user involvement, and computerized development tools. These tools may include GUI builders, Computer Aided Software Engineering (CASE) tools (in Oracle this would be Oracle Designer or a similar tool), Database Management Systems (DBMS), fourth-generation programming languages (in Oracle this may be PL/SQL), code generators (in Oracle this could be APEX, Oracle Forms, Reports, JDeveloper etc.) , and object-oriented techniques (in Oracle this would be the object-relational ability to embed code and validation properties in the database, associated with particular tables).

- Active user involvement is imperative. It generally includes a concept of joint application design (JAD), where users are intensely involved in system design, via structured workshops.

- Standard systems analysis and design methods can be fitted into a RAD framework.

- In RAD, the key emphasis is on fulfilling the business need, while technological or engineering excellence is of lesser importance.

- Project control involves prioritizing development and defining delivery deadlines or "timeboxes". If the project starts to slip, emphasis is on reducing requirements to fit the timebox, not in increasing the deadline. In a slipping schedule, non-essentials are abandoned.

- RAD attempts to reduce inherent project risk by breaking a project into smaller segments and providing more ease-of-change during the development process.

- RAD iteratively produces production software, as opposed to throwaway prototypes. Each RAD recursion is a working system. Each recursion seeks to come closer to the consensus of user requirements.

- RAD produces the documentation necessary to facilitate future development and maintenance.

Rollback: Use the ROLLBACK statement to undo work done in the current transaction, or to manually undo the work done by an in-doubt distributed transaction. If a transaction or set of transactions has been done on a set of table data, it can be reverted in the same session using the ROLLBACK command. Rollback is the transactional opposite to COMMIT.

Row-level locking: When an UPDATE statement is issued that affects a group of rows in a table; all of the affected rows are locked immediately. Of course, other processes continue to be able to read any row in the table, including the ones that are actually being updated. When other processes do read updated rows, they see only the old version of the row prior to update (via a rollback segment), until the changes are actually *committed*. This is known as a consistent read. The row level locks are held until the locking process issues either a COMMIT or ROLLBACK statement.

With row-level locking, each row within a table can be locked individually. Locked rows can be updated only by the locking process. All other rows in the table are still available for updating by other processes.

Schema: A schema is the set of objects (tables, views, indexes, etc) that belong to a user account. The word is also often used as another way to refer to an Oracle user.

Schema diagram: In database design a schema diagram is a schematic, similar to an E-R diagram. The difference is that a schema diagram shows physical database objects such as tables, views, primary and foreign keys etc., rather than logical entities and relationships.

A schema diagram is normally produced after an E-R model has been fully normalised, but before the physical database has been built. The schema diagram is a very useful tool for developers. It operates like a database "map", because it allows them to see exactly where and how data may be extracted and maintained in the physical database.

A schema diagram is produced using a tool such as Oracle Designer, (Toad and other tools also produce Schema diagrams, but none are as well integrated to the Oracle database as the Designer product).

Security data and functional: Oracle provides very granular and very safe built-in security functions, which operate at a role, user, privilege, object, row, and column level.

- **Basic User Functional Privileges:** When a user account is created, they are allocated certain group privileges. A normal operational user would be allocated so-called CONNECT privileges. This would not allow them to create private database objects such as tables, but would allow them to connect to the database as a basic user. A developer would be granted RESOURCE privilege, which allows them to use DML commands, and a DBA would receive DBA privilege, which gives them the right to create database objects and grant privileges on them to others etc.

- **Roles and Tables:** When tables have been created as part of a database build, they are only accessible to the application owner user and the DBA. No-one else has any form of access to these tables. They must first be granted explicit access to these tables to perform the explicit operations SELECT, INSERT, UPDATE, DELETE.

  So, in addition to granting users these basic roles, a database administrator and the application designer would also define and create a matrix of user roles into which all physical users would fall. For example, a role of "Invoice Entry" would

  "GRANT SELECT, INSERT, UPDATE, DELETE on INVOICE_HEADERS to INVOICE_ENTRY_ROLE"

  "GRANT SELECT, INSERT, UPDATE, DELETE on INVOICE_LINES to INVOICE_ENTRY_ROLE"

- **Roles and Users:** Any new user joining the Invoice entry team would then be granted this role and thus inherit its privileges as follows:

  "GRANT INVOICE_ENTRY_ROLE to NEW_USER"

  The effect of this would be that this user would have the right to insert, update, delete and select from the INVOICE_HEADERS and INVOICE_LINES tables.

- **Restricting Data access:** A user or role can be explicitly excluded from any or all forms of access to a particular dataset within a table, using various methods including database views or the use of Virtual Private Database (VPD). This enables you to create security policies to control database access at the row and column level. Essentially, Oracle Virtual Private Database adds a dynamic WHERE clause to a SQL statement that is issued against the table, view, or synonym to which an Oracle Virtual Private Database security policy was applied.

From these simple examples we can see that Oracle provides an extremely safe and very granular level of security. The whole subject of security is an important component in application design, and the priority is to design a simple but resilient method of administrating users which guarantees data and functional security.

SQL*Plus (SQL pronounced "Sequel"): SQL*Plus is the most basic Oracle Database utility, with a basic command-line interface. It is an Oracle product based on the ANSI standard SQL (Structured Query Language). The primary command syntax is divided into two parts:

- **DDL:** Data definition language, used to create and modify database objects, e.g. "CREATE TABLE INVOICES..."

- **DML:** Data modification language, used to INSERT, UPDATE, DELETE and SELECT from existing database objects such as tables and views etc., e.g. "SELECT * FROM INVOICES WHERE INVOICE_NO = '123456'..."

Unit and System Testing: There are several levels of software testing. Unit testing and System testing are 2 important components of a complete test regime. Other testing components may include Integration testing, Load testing, Scalability testing etc.

- **Unit testing**, also known as component testing, refers to tests that verify the functionality of a specific section of code, usually at a functional level. These types of tests are usually written by developers as they work on code to ensure that the specific function is working as expected. Unit testing alone cannot verify the functionality of a piece of software, but rather is used to assure that the building blocks the software uses work independently of each other.

- **System Testing:** System testing of software is conducted on a complete, integrated system to evaluate the system's compliance with its specified requirements. System testing falls within the scope of black box testing, and as such, should require no knowledge of the inner design of the code or logic. As a rule, system testing takes, as its input, all of the "integrated" software components that have successfully passed integration testing and also the software system itself. The purpose of integration testing is to detect any inconsistencies between the software units that are integrated together or between any of the assemblages and the hardware. System testing is a more limited type of testing; it seeks to detect defects within the system as a whole.

System testing is performed on the entire system in the context of a Functional Requirement Specification and a System Requirement Specification. System testing tests not only the design, but also the behaviour, and even the expectations of the customer. It is also intended to test up to and beyond the bounds defined in the software/hardware requirements specification.

Validation of data: Data validation is the process by which data incoming to a system is tested to ensure that it conforms to the basic business rules of the system. These business rules include low level testing of the data type (alpha or numeric), the form of the data (length etc). The validation may also include testing that data is related to an existing parent record, that the keys of a record are unique, and that columns within a record conform with various cross-validation rules, specific to the business. In Oracle, much of the data validation process is embedded in the database itself, within database primary, unique and foreign key constraints and does not need to be separately coded.

XML: Extensible Markup Language (XML) is a markup language that defines a set of rules for encoding documents in a format that is both human-readable and machine-readable. It is defined in the XML 1.0 Specification produced by the W3C, and several other related specifications, all open standards.

---o0o---

10. Other useful sources of information.

Here is a list of basic sources of information relating to Oracle and relational databases that may be useful:

Revisions and Feedback to Oracle Quick Guides:

These guides are under continuous revision and re-publication. But, if there is anything which you think we have missed or would like to comment on, please send your feedback to: admin@cornelio.es. We appreciate your input.

Oracle Main Websites:

- Oracle Main website: Oracle.com

- Oracle Technology Network: Oracle Technology Network for downloads, news and technical advice. Need to open an account.

- Oracle Technical Library - All Oracle documentation

Relational Theory - Codd

- Codd, E.F. (1970). "A Relational Model of Data for Large Shared Data Banks".

- Codd, E.F. (1970). "Relational Completeness of Data Base Sublanguages". Database Systems: 65–98. CiteSeerX: 10.1.1.86.9277.

- Codd, E.F.; Codd S.B. and Salley C.T. (1993). "Providing OLAP to User-Analysts: An IT Mandate".

- Codd, E.F. (1981-11-09). "1981 Turing Award Lecture - Relational Database: A Practical Foundation for Productivity".

Relational Theory - General

- Feasibility of a set-theoretic data structure: a general structure based on a reconstituted definition of relation (Childs' 1968 research cited by Codd's 1970 paper)

- The Third Manifesto (TTM)

- Relational Databases at the Open Directory Project

- Relational Model

- Binary relations and tuples compared with respect to the semantic web

Database Normalization:

- Database Normalization Basics by Mike Chapple (About.com)
- Database Normalization Intro, Part 2
- An Introduction to Database Normalization by Mike Hillyer.
- A tutorial on the first 3 normal forms by Fred Coulson
- DB Normalization Examples
- Description of the database normalization basics by Microsoft
- Database Normalization and Design Techniques by Barry Wise
- A Simple Guide to Five Normal Forms in Relational Database Theory

Useful Sites

- Ask Tom

---o0o---

About the Author

Malcolm Coxall, the author, is a business and IT systems analyst and consultant with more than 30 years freelance experience in Europe and the Middle East. Malcolm has worked in Oracle systems design and development for the last 25 years as a developer, business analyst, database designer, DBA, systems administrator, team lead and project manager.

With experience working for many of the world's largest corporate and institutional players, as well as for several government and international agencies, Malcolm has extensive hands-on experience in designing and building large-scale Oracle systems in many diverse vertical markets such as banking, oil, defence, telecoms, manufacturing, mining, food, agriculture, aerospace, and engineering.

Malcolm also writes and publishes books, papers and articles on human system design, sociology, environmental economics, sustainable technology and technology in environmental protection and food production.

Malcolm's company designed and built the Oracle systems known as BioTrack and EcoBase. BioTrack is an integrated agriculture and food production control and traceability system designed specifically for organic and other specially controlled food production industries. EcoBase is an environmental research database for bringing together environmental data with complex statistical analysis techniques. Both of these systems were designed and developed in Oracle 10g and are commercialised as cloud-based systems directly available to end-users.

Malcolm lives in southern Spain from where he continues his free-lance Oracle consultancy and his writing, whilst managing the family's organic farm.

---o0o---

www.ingramcontent.com/pod-product-compliance
Lightning Source LLC
La Vergne TN
LVHW052312060326
832902LV00021B/3837